394
BRA

Braine, Susan

Drumbeat ...
heartbeat

$19.95                               21533

| DATE | | | |
|---|---|---|---|
| | | | |
| | | | |
| | | | |
| | | | |
| | | | |
| | | | |
| | | | |
| | | | |
| | | | |
| | | | |
| | | | |
| | | | |
| | | | |

# DRUMBEAT... HEARTBEAT

# DRUMBEAT ··· HEARTBEAT

## A
## Celebration of
## the Powwow

**Text and Photographs by Susan Braine**

 Lerner Publications Company ● Minneapolis

# Author's Note

Powwows happen all over the United States, and many tribes of Indian people participate. Although clothing, dance, and music styles differ from one area to another, most of the dances and songs you see and hear at a powwow come from either the Southern or the Northern Plains tribes. The text and photographs in this book emphasize the Northern Plains style of dancing. Northern Plains tribes include Blackfeet, Assiniboine, Lakota, Dakota, Crow, Northern Arapaho, and Northern Cheyenne.

Series Editor: Gordon Regguinti
Series Consultants: W. Roger Buffalohead, Juanita G. Corbine Espinosa

The photograph on page 7 is by Don Suppes. The photograph on page 23 is by Catherine Whipple.

*This book is available in two editions:*
Library binding by Lerner Publications Company
Soft cover by First Avenue Editions
241 First Avenue North
Minneapolis, MN 55401

LIBRARY OF CONGRESS CATALOGING-IN-PUBLICATION DATA

Braine, Susan.
    Drumbeat . . . heartbeat : a celebration of the powwow / Susan Braine.
      p. cm.
    Includes bibliographical references.
    ISBN 0-8225-2656-5 (library binding)
    ISBN 0-8225-9711-X (paperback)
    1. Powwows—Juvenile literature. 2. Indians of North America—Rites and ceremonies—Juvenile literature. 3. Indians of North America—Social life and customs—Juvenile literature. I. Title.
E98.P86B73   1995
394—dc20                                      94-42594
                                                   CIP

Manufactured in the United States of America
1  2  3  4  5  6 - I/JR - 00  99  98  97  96  95

*Dedicated to the memory of
my beautiful Assiniboine mother and friend,
Christine Elizabeth (Cain) Braine
11/9/14 – 11/3/90*

## *Preface*

I just love the powwow! In fact, I'm preparing right this minute to go home to Lame Deer, Montana, for the annual Fourth of July Northern Cheyenne Powwow. I just bought a new powwow chair (a folding lawn chair) and a new tent.

It will take me two days to drive from Lincoln, Nebraska, where I work, to Lame Deer. I haven't been home since last summer. I can't wait to feel the drum pounding with my every heartbeat. I used to go to sleep every night to that sound. Old Man Red Woman, who lived up the road from our family, sang to the drum every night. Especially on summer nights when all the windows were open, it sounded like he was right in the middle of my bedroom.

I also can't wait to see my family. My son Scott and his wife, Holly, are driving down from Anchorage in their pickup truck, and my oldest son, KC, is trying to scrape up enough money to fly in. Unfortunately, my youngest son, Martin, can't make it this year. My friend Nan from New York City is coming, and so is Kirby, from across the state in Hamilton, Montana. Teddy said he'd try to make it. I wonder if Joyce and Rosalie will be there? It'll be so good to see all the family and friends—the thought of it helped me through a long winter. And I can already taste that mouthwatering taco meat, cheese, lettuce, and tomatoes heaped on a big, fat, round piece of fry bread!

Butch and Lena told me they would have the sweat lodge ready. They know how much it means to me to make that spiritual connection to the homeland where I grew up. The sweat lodge is a very special place to go to pray.

There are many, many Indians like me who choose to live and work away from the place where our families and hearts are. Many of us make it a priority to go back home to visit and replenish the soul. I can understand why the great gray whales and the salmon travel miles and miles to return to the same spot year after year!

If you gain nothing more from this book than an appreciation that some things in life are *good,* I will consider it successful. A powwow is one of those good things in life.

The powwow, besides creating a better understanding between Indian people and non-Indian people who enjoy the celebration, gives me a feeling of pride. I love to see my people working together, enjoying themselves, and lookin' good. I love being with my family and friends. I love seeing old traditions being kept alive.

*Susan Braine*

Check out a powwow sometime. There are thousands of these celebrations throughout the country every year. You'll love it too!

—*Susan Braine*

Close your eyes and imagine your heart pounding to the beat of the drum. Imagine long buckskin fringes swaying to the rhythm of the dance. Think about fluffy feathers in every color of the rainbow swirling and bobbing. Listen to the tinkling of a hundred tin jingles. Smell the dust kicked up by dancing feet and the faint scent of foods—Indian tacos, corn soup, and fry bread, as well as hamburgers, hot dogs, popcorn, and cotton candy. Where can you see, hear, and smell these things? On the sidelines of the dance arena at a Native American powwow. Or perhaps you're out there in the middle, dancing!

We dance to give thanks. We dance to celebrate and share our ancient cultures with each other. We dance to meet old and new friends. We honor each other, and we honor the spirits of our ancestors and the loved ones we've lost. We honor animals and birds by wearing costumes made of skins and feathers and dancing in imitation of them.

The heartbeat of the drum unites many different nations of Native people, and non-Natives as well. The beating of the drum is the center of what we call the powwow. A powwow is a way for Indian people to keep our traditions alive. It is also a reunion with family and friends.

The meaning of the word *powwow* has changed over the last two hundred years. In the Algonquian Indian languages, a "pau-wau" was a conjurer or medicine man, and pau-wauing meant to perform a religious curing ceremony. The term was used in a new way in the 1800s—mainly by non-Indians—to describe just about any gathering of Indian people, whether it was a war dance or a victory celebration, a social get-together or a meeting to discuss some important topic.

The word *powwow,* like many other Indian words in the English language, was adopted by Indians and non-Indians alike. Even tribes who do not speak an Algonquian language now use the word to announce a social get-together, a celebration of Indian culture. All who wish to attend are invited.

Powwows take place all over the United States and Canada and sometimes even in Europe and the Far East. They are held just about anywhere you can imagine—in a school gymnasium, on a reservation, or in an auditorium in a large city.

Although there are a few powwows throughout the year—on Veterans Day, Christmas, and New Year's Day, for example—summertime is the height of the powwow season. In most areas of the country, the powwow season starts on Memorial Day and ends on Labor Day. People who spend the summer traveling from one powwow to another refer to the season as "the powwow trail." These people are most likely food and crafts vendors, or very good dancers! Some dancers travel miles and miles to attend powwows all over the country. They compete in contests in which thousands of dollars in prizes might be offered.

Many powwows also host all-Indian rodeos, sponsored by the Indian Rodeo Cowboys Association. To qualify in the Indian National Finals Rodeo, Indian cowboys must compete in a number of rodeos. Some Indian cowboys are also excellent powwow dancers and compete in both events. Phil Whiteman Jr., a Northern Cheyenne from Lame Deer, Montana, has been known to ride a bucking bronco in the rodeo arena and then dance half an hour later at the powwow area!

Most people's favorite place to attend a powwow is on an Indian reservation, at a place set aside by the tribe as the powwow grounds. The grounds are usually outdoors, with plenty of room for people to set up tent and tipi camps. The tribe that owns the property tries to make camping comfortable for visitors.

A large part of the fun of going to a powwow is camping out. Powwow visitors and dancers who plan to camp usually arrive the evening before the powwow begins. When they get there, they look for other friends or family who have already set up camp. Some families camp in the same place year after year, even leaving their tipi poles or tent frames on the campsite.

The food and crafts vendors usually camp next to their booths. The people who sell food pay a daily fee to the powwow committee (members of the tribe who organize the powwow) to help cover the costs of electricity and water. Food vendors also have to pass a public health inspection, just like a restaurant or cafe that serves food to the public, to ensure that the food preparation areas are clean and the food is properly refrigerated.

There are also booths reserved for people from different tribes to sell their artwork and supplies such as leather, feathers, tanned animal hides, and beads.

Top: *Jewelry and crafts vendors display their wares along the sidelines at powwows.* Bottom: *Food vendors sell fry bread, Indian tacos, hamburgers, and snacks.*

For many Indian people, the annual powwow is the only time they see certain friends and family members during the year. Thousands of Native American people do not live on an Indian reservation. On most reservations, there are not enough jobs to support all the tribal members, so some people move to cities to find work. Many reservations do not have opportunities for higher education, so tribal members who want to go to college must leave the reservation.

*Powwows bring together friends and families.*

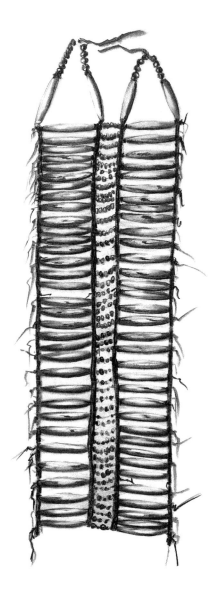

A typical day at a powwow on a reservation starts when the powwow coordinator or the announcer wakes everyone up over the loudspeaker. He or she says what time it is and gives a rundown of the day's events, adding funny comments such as, "Luke Warmwater, you're wanted at the showers."

A good powwow announcer is highly valued, because the job requires a lot of knowledge about the dances and music, not to mention the skills necessary to keep a powwow moving. It is up to the announcer to make sure that everyone knows what's going on, especially the dancers. The announcer must be highly organized and have a good sense of "Indian humor." A few popular, top-notch announcers, like Wallace Coffey, president of the Comanche Nation, and Dr. Dale Old Horn from the Crow Nation, are kept very busy during the powwow season.

At some powwows, an Indian honor guard, who is a military veteran, hoists Old Glory (the American flag) up the flagpole early in the morning. At other powwows, such as the Crow Fair and Rodeo, there is a huge parade through the powwow grounds each morning. People rise early, eat, and groom and decorate their horses for the event. Men, women, and children in their finest beadwork, buckskins, and feathers line up for the parade, some riding beautiful ponies.

*The Crow Fair and Rodeo, in Crow Agency, Montana, starts with a colorful parade.*

At the opening ceremonies of a powwow, the dancers enter the arena in a spectacular showing of their unique dress. This is called the grand entry. The dancers line up according to their styles of dance and follow the military veterans, who carry the flags of the United States. Flags of different Indian nations or the flags of Canada or the state where the powwow is held might be flown.

The grand entry lets everyone know that the powwow is about to begin. The spectators take their places around the arbor (the center of the grounds) to watch. All the dancers proceed into the arbor behind the flag bearers, eventually forming a huge circle inside the dance area. The spectators get to see how many dancers will compete in the contest dancing, because the contestants usually participate in the grand entry.

All the spectators stand for the grand entry, and the host drum group plays the flag song, which is the Indian version of the national anthem. Every powwow has a drum group that helps to sponsor the powwow. That group is called the host drum.

Following the veterans into the dance area are local and visiting tribal officials, state politicians, powwow queens and princesses, and other honored guests. Next come all the different categories of dancers—male traditional dancers, female traditional dancers, men's fancy dancers, women's fancy shawl dancers, grass dancers, jingle dress dancers, and the gourd dancers. The contestants wear a number. They have paid an entry fee to be eligible for the contest dances. Other dancers, who do not enter the contests, dance simply because they enjoy it.

After all the dancers have entered the arena or arbor, they stand at attention until the flags are presented and the flag song is over. Most of the time, an elder or a spiritual leader offers a prayer to the Creator. Then everyone dances out of the arbor—and the powwow is underway.

You can tell the male traditional dancers from the rest because they are dressed in deerskins (sometimes with a cloth shirt) and adorned with eagle, hawk, and other bird feather bustles attached to their backs (the feathers are not dyed). Most male traditional dancers wear a headdress, such as an eagle-feather bonnet, a coyote head, or a roach, which is made from the long hairs of a porcupine and decorated with a dyed red deer tail. Many dancers go bare-legged, but some wear cloth or deerskin leggings and a breechcloth, as well as bells around the ankles and moccasins. Their dance is quiet and stately.

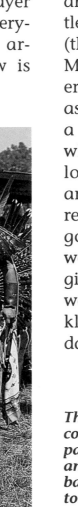

*The men's traditional dance comes from a time when war parties returned to the village and danced out the story of a battle, or returning hunters told how they tracked their prey.*

The female traditional dancers usually wear long, beaded buckskin dresses with long fringes on the sleeves and fringes around the hem. They wear decorated leggings and deerskin moccasins. These women carry a shawl over one arm and usually hold a fan made from an eagle wing in the other hand. Their hair is braided and they wear colorful beaded barrettes or headbands. Some women, whose tribal beliefs allow it, wear a single breath feather (a soft, downy feather) from an eagle, tied in their hair behind an ear. The women's traditional dancers move very gracefully and slowly.

*The women's traditional dance consists of very small movements. The women bend their knees and turn slightly.*

21

The fancy dancers wear the most colorful clothing and show the most energy in their dancing. They shake their shoulders and legs and use incredibly fancy footwork. Fancy dancing is probably the kind of Indian dancing most familiar to non-Indians. This dance style evolved from the early Plains tribes' victory or war dances. The showman Buffalo Bill Cody exploited these dances, hiring Indians to dance in his Wild West Show. Fancy dancing is gaining more respect within the Indian community, but there was a time when anyone who participated in this style of dance was considered a "sellout" to the white society.

Most fancy shawl dancers are young women with lots of energy. Their dresses are made of cloth, and they often wear matching leggings. The moccasins are beaded to match the dress. What distinguishes these young women are their long-fringed shawls, which snap and sway to their fast footwork. Sometimes all you can see are twirling legs and flying shawls, like great birds dancing.

The grass dancers say that theirs is the oldest style of Indian dancing. Their costumes are made of layered fringes of brightly colored yarn. In the past, grass or feathers were used instead of yarn. The grass dancers imitate prairie chickens or other birds, dipping low to the ground and circling in a crouch. They wear porcupine roaches on their heads.

*Because it comes from the Omaha tribe, the grass dance is sometimes called the Omaha dance.*

24

Left: *Gourd dancers*

The noisiest of all dancers are the jingle dress dancers. The noise comes from hundreds of jingles, which have been cut from tin snuff-can lids and shaped into cones, then sewn in rows or patterns on dresses. Most jingle dress dancers are young women. They like to travel in pairs or in a group, making their entrance known to all within hearing distance! Their active dance is mostly twisting and turning.

The gourd dancers hold rattles made of gourds, which they shake as they move.

*The jingle dress dance first appeared in the dream of an Ojibway holy man.*

25

The center of every powwow is the drum. The drum is like the heartbeat of a Native nation. The drum and all its parts are sacred and must be treated with respect. Drummers consider it a special gift from the Creator to be able to play the drum and sing. When the drum beats, Native people know that a celebration is to follow or that a ceremony is being conducted.

A drum group is made up of as many drummers as can fit comfortably around the drum. At smaller powwows, there may be only a few drum groups, and they all take turns drumming for each dance. At the larger powwows, there are usually a lot of drum groups. They also take turns, unless a certain drum group is requested. It is a great honor to be specially asked to drum. The people who make the request are expected to pay the drum group a small sum of money.

Most drummers are men, but sometimes you will see a woman in a drum group and, very rarely, an all-women's drum group. Most often women stand behind the drum, singing along. According to the traditional beliefs of some tribes, women cannot drum, because the gift of drumming was given to men only, just as some gifts, such as beadwork, were given to women only.

People form drum groups with friends or relatives who also like to sing and drum. They get together and practice, eventually traveling together to powwows. The powwow committee usually provides money to help with travel expenses for visiting drum groups. Each drum group is assigned a number. When the announcer calls their number, they are the next to drum. The host drum is given the number one, and they sit in the honored spot closest to the announcer's stand.

*For many people, the drum symbolizes the heartbeat. In some Native cultures, the drum also represents thunder.*

If you've been to a powwow, you probably noticed a group of spectators who rushed with their tape recorders to the drum group that was going to play next. Many of these people like to record the music for their own listening enjoyment. Others are dancers who tape the songs so they can learn them.

Some drum groups play trick songs that cause a dancer to miss a beat, so dancers must learn the songs of each group very well. The dancers must start at just the right time and their last step must match the last beat of the drum.

The drum groups play many different kinds of Indian music. Some songs are very old traditional songs and some are new. Each drum group develops their own style, depending on what tribe they're from. Most powwow drum groups play Northern style songs, which originally came from Northern Plains tribes such as the Lakota, Crow, Assiniboine, and Blackfeet. Northern style singing is higher than in the south. Each song is sung four times, because four is a sacred number in Indian belief.

Some songs have no words, and others have vocables. These are syllables without meaning that carry the melody. Other songs have words in a Native language or in English.

*Shawn Old Mouse is a young drummer from Lame Deer, Montana.*

*While many powwow dances originated in the Plains tribes, Indian people all over the country created unique dances, such as the Navajo squaw dance.*

Southern tribes have their own singing and dancing styles. For instance, the Navajo have a couples dance called the squaw dance. Other Arizona tribes, such as the Tohono O'odham (Papago) and the Pima, dance the chicken scratch, which includes accordion and sometimes guitar music, hinting at Mexican influence. The Cherokee and Creek Nations of Oklahoma like to do the stomp dance, and in Alaska, the Athabascan Indians dance the red river jig to fiddle music played in a style originally learned from the Hudson Bay Company traders and trappers, many of whom came from Scotland. But the singing is in the Athabascan language.

It's time for the first contest dance! The emcee stands behind the microphone in the announcer's booth and the arena director and judges are all ready.

Little feet in moccasins shuffle into the dance area, some hesitating, with a parent urging them forward. Some children are bashful, others are scared, and some proudly step out. It's the tiny tots contest. There are little traditional dancers with porcupine roaches bobbing on their heads and baby girls wrapped in fringed shawls, some barely able to walk yet, with their dresses hiding Pampers underneath.

*Misty McCormick, left, and Deanna Spotted Elk have fun at the Ashland Labor Day Powwow in Ashland, Montana.*

Some kids dance their hearts out, while younger ones stand and watch, tapping a toe or bobbing their heads to the drumbeat. Eventually they all start dancing, except for the ones who are scared and crying for their parents.

When the dance is over, the emcee calls them to the announcer's booth and hands out a crisp dollar bill to all the participants. The little ones who cried and would not dance are pushed forward by a parent or older brother or sister to receive their dollar. Then you see big smiles as they run back to their families.

*These dancers are from the northwest coast of the United States. Their clothing is different from the Plains style outfits.*

Next the emcee calls for an intertribal. That means all dancers may dance. It is not a contest dance.

"Drum number 10. It's a round dance," announces the emcee. Some people scurry to drum number 10 to record the song.

The round dance is a favorite for non-Indians, because it's easy to follow and they feel encouraged to participate. Everyone holds hands in a big circle. Sometimes when there are too many people for one circle, a second circle is formed outside the first so that everyone can take part. The second circle moves in the opposite direction of the first. Sometimes the circles face each other, and the dancers shake hands with each other as they go around the circle.

Many round dance songs are sung in English. Some are very funny, while some are serious or sad. Round dance songs are called 49 songs. One story goes that they come from the World War II era, when 50 Indian men from different tribes were in boot camp together. They were lonesome for home and their families. Since none of them could speak each other's native tongue, they made up songs in English and sang together whenever they could. They all vowed to meet up after the war and sing their songs again. Forty-nine soldiers from this group made it back from the war.

The contest dancing is conducted in a variety of different ways, depending on the number of dancers in each category—men's traditional, shawl, and so on. If there are too many dancers, they go through a process of elimination until the final dance-offs, which are usually held the last day of the powwow. A typical prize for winning a contest such as the men's traditional dance is $300 to $500.

Many powwows have "specials," which are contests sponsored by individual people rather than by the powwow committee. A special might pay as much as $1,000 to the winner!

Native American celebrations nearly always have spiritual meaning and elements. For example, at a powwow, if an eagle feather accidentally falls off someone's costume, the dance stops until a traditional ceremony is performed right then and there. Eagles are very sacred to Native people, and an eagle feather is treated as a fallen warrior whose spirit must be taken care of. Only people who have earned the right to touch the feather may perform the ceremony. This is usually a military veteran who has earned honors in battle. After the ceremony is performed, the person tells the story of why he or she is entitled to rescue the feather. That person is rewarded with a small sum of money by the family who "lost" the feather.

Sometimes members of medicine clans will come into the dance circle and dance, which is a great honor for everyone because the dance is then considered a blessing. (Simply defined, medicine clans are people who take care of the spiritual well-being of the tribe.) Many people go up to the medicine dancers afterward and give them money to show their appreciation for the blessing.

Some Native dancing is strictly for ceremonial purposes and is not considered social. You will not see ceremonial dancing at a powwow. In most tribal ceremonies, people watching the ceremony derive a spiritual benefit or blessing from the Creator. But only those participating in the ceremony are allowed to dance.

Most tribes have sacred ceremonials. The sun dance, for instance, is one of the ceremonial dances practiced by a number of Northern Plains tribes (Dakota, Lakota, Northern Cheyenne, Arapaho, Crow). It is a complicated four-day prayer ceremony to renew the earth and everything on it.

34

Back at the camps, families are cooking, eating, and visiting. Children ride horseback or play or nap. Those who plan to dance are getting their clothing ready.

Austin and Denise Littlesun help their children prepare their outfits, which they made by hand. Baby Shusden toddles around, losing one legging as his mother tries to supervise the dressing of the other six children.

Gathering all the materials necessary for making the outfits takes a lot of time and costs a lot of money. Some things, such as eagle or other feathers, tanned deerskins, porcupine guard hairs, and white-tail deer tails, are hard to find.

Many of the birds and animals that Indians have used in cultural activities for centuries are now protected by the federal government. It is illegal for non-Indians to possess many items from these animals, but some Indians are allowed to keep them, because of the Indian Religious Freedom Act.

Austin Littlesun works as a jail guard for the Northern Cheyenne Tribal Police Department, and Denise is a parent trainer for the Head Start program on the Northern Cheyenne Indian Reservation. They live in Lame Deer, Montana, the tribal headquarters. Their children go to a public school in Colstrip, a town about 20 miles from the reservation.

*A porcupine roach dazzles the eye.*

During winter evenings, the Littlesuns get out their dance outfits and make repairs or design new items. The family members have their own drum group, so they also use this time to practice drumming and make up new songs that they will sing during the powwow season.

Now that it's powwow season, the Littlesuns, like many Indian families, travel to as many powwows as they can. Sometimes it's hard for Austin to get time off from his job.

*The Littlesun family members make up their own drum group.*

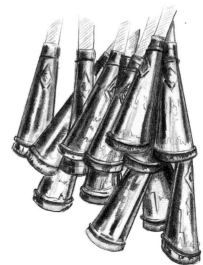

Besides the dancing, another important part of a powwow is the *giveaway*, especially at the local powwows that are held on reservations. A giveaway pays tribute to someone. Instead of giving gifts to that person, however, the person's family gives gifts to many other people. Giveaways are usually held during the early afternoon, in between intertribal dances.

Families give things away in honor of someone, usually a member of their family, for a variety of reasons. Giving away valuable items shows, first of all, humbleness to the Creator. It is also a sign of the family's pride in the person being honored, and it shows generosity, a highly prized virtue.

Giveaways may be held for someone in the family who just graduated from college, for someone who was honorably discharged from the military—especially if the person survived a war, such as Desert Storm—in honor of a young woman who finished a reign as a powwow queen or princess, or for an Indian cowboy who won at the Indian National Finals Rodeo.

Many giveaways take place a year after a family member dies, marking the end of the mourning period. But these are not the only reasons for a giveaway. You can learn the reason for a giveaway by listening to what is said about the person who is being honored.

*Family members honor a deceased relative at a giveaway by carrying pictures of him.*

The giveaway always starts out with a song for the person being honored. That person leads the dancing, unless the giveaway is for someone who has died. In that case, a family member carries a picture of the deceased person. As the family circles around the arbor during the honor song, they are joined by friends who also wish to pay tribute to the person. When the honor song is finished, the family begins the giveaway.

Many different things may be given away. If a bridle or halter is given, it means that the person will also receive a horse. Sometimes the horse itself is led into the arena and given away. A horse is a traditional gift from the days when almost everyone had horses. Long ago, a prized buffalo horse was the ultimate gift. (A buffalo horse was specially trained to run very fast and very close to a buffalo's left side so a hunter riding the horse could shoot his arrow into the buffalo's heart.) Nowadays, the finest gift is a "table gift." It consists of a tablecloth, dishes, silverware, and cooking utensils (sometimes with food prepared inside the pots and pans), canned goods, fresh vegetables and fruits, bread, meat, yard goods (sewing material), blankets, and shawls. Some families prepare many table gifts. There are usually beautiful handmade fringed shawls, star quilts, and wool blankets heaped on top of a table.

*After hearing her name called, Auntie Thelma walks across the arbor to receive a gift.*

*Children eagerly pick up candy thrown on the ground at a giveaway.*

If the person being honored is young (or someone who loves or loved children), the family may throw money and candy into the arena. All the children in the crowd are allowed to run out and keep whatever they find.

Sometimes, during the honor song, when the person being recognized is dancing, a member of the family spreads a blanket or shawl on the ground. After the person dances on it, the shawl is left for whomever rushes out to claim it.

The people who receive gifts have usually helped the person being honored at some time in his or her lifetime. The family knows most of the people they plan to give a gift to, but sometimes they set aside a certain number of gifts to give to visitors from far away, or they may call for anyone from a specific tribe to receive a gift.

Many years ago, two traditional, respected families on the Fort Peck Reservation in Montana were having giveaways. Both families prepared wall tents (big tents that have four walls and look like little houses) filled with all the things necessary for setting up housekeeping, including a stove, dishes, beds, and food. Each family thought that their gesture was the most generous—until the person who received one of the tents pulled up the wooden stakes that held the tent down and discovered a silver dollar under each stake!

*A blanket laid on the ground is meant to be given away.*

When all the contest dancing is finished, the powwow is over. By now it is probably late in the evening or even early in the morning! Some people spend the night in camp, and others pack up and hit the road as soon as the dancing is over. Those staying will take down the tents and tipis the next day and be on their way. By the end of that day, the powwow grounds will be left with only a whisper of the hustle and bustle. There may be a few tents still up, tipi poles leaning against a cottonwood tree, and workers cleaning up the grounds.

If you have attended a powwow, for days afterward you will remember the flurry of activity, the excitement of the contest dancing, the feeling of warmth from being surrounded by family and close friends, the beauty of many different dance outfits, and the beadwork, porcupine quillwork, and eagle feathers.

You will remember the beating of the drum in time with your heartbeat.

# Word List

**band**—a group of people within a larger tribe, or group, of Indians

**bustle**—a cluster of feathers that are attached to a person's back

**drum group**—a group of people who form a circle around one large drum and play it

**elder**—an older person who is respected and admired for his or her knowledge and experience

**fry bread**—light, fluffy bread that is deep-fried

**giveaway**—the giving of gifts to many people in honor of someone

**grand entry**—a procession of all the dancers in a powwow into the arena or arbor

**honor guard**—a military veteran who carries and raises the American flag at a powwow

**honor song**—a song played by a drum group during a giveaway, in honor of the person being recognized, or the flag song, which is the Indian version of the national anthem

**host drum**—a drum group that is chosen by the powwow's sponsors

**intertribal**—a dance in which anyone can participate

**jingles**—small cone-shaped pieces of metal, usually made by turning snuff-can lids into cones

**medicine clan**—a tribe's spiritual leaders

**powwow**—a celebration of Indian culture that includes dancing and drumming

**reservation**—an area of land that Indian people kept through agreement with the United States government

**roach**—a man's headdress made of long porcupine hairs, which resembles a horse's mane that has been clipped short

**round dance**—a dance in which participants join hands and move in a circle

## *For Further Reading*

Ancona, George. *Powwow.* San Diego: Harcourt Brace Jovanovich, 1993.

Crum, Robert. *Eagle Drum: On the Powwow Trail with a Young Grass Dancer.* New York: Four Winds Press, 1994.

King, Sandra. *Shannon: An Ojibway Dancer.* Minneapolis: Lerner Publications, 1993.

*Powwow: Questions and Answers.* Available from United Tribes Technical College, Office of Public Information, 3315 University Drive, Bismarck, ND 58504.

Roberts, Chris. *Powwow Country.* Helena, MT: American & World Geographic Publications, 1992.

# *About the Contributors*

**Susan Braine** is a member of the Assiniboine Tribe, Fort Peck Reservation, in Montana. Her great-grand-mother, Josephine Waggoner, a Hunkpapa Dakota from the Standing Rock Reservation in North Dakota, was a writer, poet, and artist at the turn of the century. Braine was born at Crow Agency, Montana, and grew up on the Northern Cheyenne Reservation. Braine has managed public radio stations in New Mexico, North Dakota, and Alaska and served as executive producer for "National Native News." Currently Braine is manager of American Indian Radio on Satellite, a radio programming service covering Native issues. The service is delivered via satellite to 25 Native-owned public radio stations in the United States. In addition to her work in radio, Braine has been a photographer and writer for many years. She lives in Lincoln, Nebraska, and has three grown sons.

Series Editor **Gordon Regguinti** is a member of the Leech Lake Band of Ojibway. He was raised on Leech Lake Reservation by his mother and grandparents. His Ojibway heritage has remained a central focus of his professional life. A graduate of the University of Minnesota with a B.A. in Indian Studies, Regguinti has written about Native American issues for newspapers and school curricula. He served as editor of the Twin Cities Native newspaper *The Circle* for two years and as executive director of the Native American Journalists Association. He lives in Minneapolis and has six children and one grandchild.

Series Consultant **W. Roger Buffalohead**, Ponca, has been involved in Indian Education for more than 20 years, serving as a national consultant on issues of Indian curricula and tribal development. He has a B.A. in American History from Oklahoma State University and an M.A. from the University of Wisconsin, Madison. Buffalohead has taught at the University of Cincinnati, the University of California, Los Angeles, and the University of Minnesota, where he was director of the American Indian Learning and Resources Center. Currently he teaches at the Institute of American Indian Arts in Santa Fe, New Mexico. Among his many activities, Buffalohead is a founding board member of the National Indian Education Association and a member of the Cultural Concerns Committee of the National Conference of American Indians. He lives in Santa Fe.

Series Consultant **Juanita G. Corbine Espinosa**, Dakota/Ojibway, is the director of Native Arts Circle, Minnesota's first statewide Native American arts agency. She is first and foremost a community organizer, active in a broad range of issues, many of which are related to the importance of art in community life. In addition, she is a board member of the Minneapolis American Indian Center and an advisory member of the Minnesota State Arts Board's Cultural Pluralism Task Force. She was one of the first people to receive the state's McKnight Human Service Award. She lives in Minneapolis.

Illustrator **Carly Bordeau** is a member of the Anishinabe nation, White Earth, Minnesota. She is a freelance graphic designer, illustrator, and photographer and the owner of All Nite Design and Photography. Carly graduated from the College of Associated Arts in St. Paul with a B.A. in Communication Design. She lives in St. Paul.